# BEYOND MOTIVATION!

*From America's Leading Teen Expert*

# BEYOND MOTIVATION!

*Why Teens Seem Disconnected and What You Can Do About It*

Yahya Bakkar

*"Beyond Motivation is powerful, inspiring, and compelling piece that SPEAKS up-close-and-personal about a sensitive topic. Yahya definitely knows what he's doing."*
–Royce Addington, Entrepreneur

*"A must read for parents and teachers looking to make a difference. Yahya breaks it down so that his message is very simple to understand. He offers an outstanding perspective on what teens, parents and teachers go through. I highly recommend this book."*
–Mustafa Elbaf , Strategic Interventionist

*"Beyond Motivation allowed me to "get over myself" as Yahya says in his book and help my son with his own struggle with ADHD. Reading this book was exactly what I needed to do to help raise my 10 year old son who will soon be a teenager."*
–Sheryl Magpali, Parent

*"I found your book to be a powerful tool in connecting even more to my children. It should be on every parent's shelf."*
–Judith N., Mother of two teenagers

*"Brilliant! This book blew me away! If you deal with teenagers, get this book now. You'll thank me later."*

–Arzu B., Mother of a teenager

*"I have 8 kids of my own ages 5-25. I have GREAT relationships with each one of them. I agree whole-heartedly all that Yahya is advocating in his book. It is entirely about developing and maintaining healthy and positive relationships with teens through compassion and empathy. Their behavior, academic achievement all hinge on the adults who show they care by loving them unconditionally and make time to listen to them, (not necessarily agreeing with them), who provide a safe non critical zone in which they can open up in and who believe in them. Yahya explains this very clearly and passionately having lived this experience. This little book should be spread far and wide to help bridge the generation gaps and heal hurting parents, teachers and teens."*

–Sophie Lejeune Barcant, Love and
Logic Parenting Facilitator

*"Every school, parent, teacher and teen can benefit from Yahya's work. I wish he was around when I was growing up!"*

–Susan Russo—Author, Speaker, Divorce Coach

Beyond Motivation!

Also by Yahya Bakkar

## Books

### *The Ultimate Guide to Teen life*

## Keynote/Workshop Programs

***Teen Life Matters-Keynote*** (45-60 minutes) Not only do teenagers need to know that their lives are valuable, they also must understand that they will go through difficult, confusing and hurtful times. Yahya reminds his audience that every choice they make within those moments will inevitably create their future and it's up to them to make sure it's an unforgettable one.

*For teens and young adults. Ideal for middle schools, high schools, student leadership organizations and non-profit organizations.*

***Teen Life 101-Workshop:*** (45-60 minutes) Based on *The Ultimate Guide to Teen Life*, students will learn the 15 life lessons to create an amazing future.

*For teens and young adults. Ideal for middle schools, high schools, student leadership organizations and non-profit organizations*

***The Bullying Cure:*** **(45-60 minutes)** Most anti-bullying programs fail in targeting the root cause of the problem. Our nationwide program is dedicated to transform bullies into positive leaders.

***Beyond Motivation-Keynote/Workshop: (45-60 minutes)*** Learn how to apply all the information in this book and more through a live and interactive setting.

*For parents, educators and mental health professionals.*

For more information about workshops, programs and coaching, visit:

www.NationalYouthSpeaker.com
www.TheBullyingCure.com

# Beyond Motivation!

*Why Teens Seem Disconnected and
What You Can Do About It*

Copyright © 2012 by: Yahya Bakkar.

ISBN-13: 978-1469984216

Printed in United States of America

*This book is dedicated to all the families who love their children, teachers who genuinely care for their students, mental health professionals who go out of their way to find better solutions and to each individual who is serving as a positive role model for the next generations.*

*Thank you for allowing me to serve you. I unconditionally appreciate your trust as well as support.*

# Table of Contents

# Disclaimer

*B*EFORE YOU BEGIN *absorbing the awesome knowledge from Yahya's University of Wisdom (the world's #1 invisible university) please understand that I am BY NO MEANS a health professional. I share my advice and perspective based on my experience and education as a youth motivational speaker, lifestyle coach, student, child, and my knowledge instilled by the top experts in the field of personal development and human behavior. If something doesn't resonate with you, by all means, don't use it. If something makes sense, apply it in your life immediately. In other words, take what works and throw out what doesn't. Also to make things easier, I will use the word teen or teenager interchangeably with student. Now, let us begin!*

# Purpose of this Book

*"When you're at your best, your children will be more successful in school, at home, and in life."*
*Fern Weis, Parent Coach*

Our adolescent years are probably the most challenging, confusing and vulnerable years of our entire lives. Yet, somewhere down the road we seem to forget that. Not because we want to, but because we simply grow up too fast and become caught up with the daily responsibilities of being an adult. In all fairness, this is not anyone's fault. It's the way our reality is set up at the moment. Trying to balance work, family, bills, raising children and living the life you've always wanted becomes a juggling act. It can feel like a huge weight being put on your shoulders. No wonder you have so much lower back and neck pain. Go get a massage. You deserve it!

But seriously, there is a huge problem today and we must try to find a sustainable solution. With the collapse of the economy and a time of uncertainty, we must challenge ourselves to prepare for a better future by being greater role models for our young ones. Since you're reading this book you have already volunteered to be in this position. You are also probably searching for better ways to strengthen the relationship with your teens or students so you can reach them more effectively. It doesn't matter if they are found inside or outside a classroom environment; what does matter is that you are a role model in their eyes. This means you must find ways to effectively connect with them to make sure they are moving in a positive direction. Once you make the connection teenagers will not only respect you, but will admire you for the rest of their lives.

**Do any of these questions sound familiar to you?**

- Why isn't my student motivated?

- How do I motivate everyone in my classroom to learn?

- Why doesn't my son/daughter listen to me when I ask them to clean up their room?

- How can I help my teen do better for themselves without sounding so uptight?

- Why are they constantly lying rather than being honest?

- Is there a way I can tell my son/daughter how I feel and what I think is right without sounding overprotective?

- How can I give my teen confidence to overcome bullying and peer pressure?

- Why is my son/daughter/student being a bully?

- Why can't they show me some respect?

These are some interesting questions that parents and teachers all over the world ask me. And what I've noticed is that behind each question there is a sense of frustration and confusion that motivates them to find quick fix solutions to end their problems. You are not here to look for a quick fix solution. You are here to build a sustainable relationship with your teens so that they will remember you for the rest of their lives as a person who has made a lasting and positive impact. This book is my attempt to address these problems while providing a fresh perspective as well as a sense of self-reliance throughout your journey helping our future leaders. Also, it is a way of partnering up with you to make sure your teens uncover what is possible for them to achieve in their lives. Please understand that what I share in this book isn't the answer to all of your challenges. It's just another point of view that can possibly shed some light upon your situation.

All the strategies, techniques and tools in the world mean nothing unless you truly understand the other person's perspective. With that being said, I hope you digest all the information that this book contains. It is short for a reason. So I invite you to absorb the material quickly and apply the knowledge into your life as you see fit. If you have any questions regarding the book or my speaking and coaching programs, please don't hesitate to visit www.NationalYouthSpeaker.com. Enjoy the journey!

# Introduction

IMAGINE YOU ARE standing on a rim of a giant canyon. On the far side are your teenage mutant ninja humans. As you look across it feels like there is no way to reach them. They communicate with each other easily using text messaging and social networks, yet when we try to communicate with them they seem inaccessible. They listen to iPods for hours but when you try to speak to them . . . they can't hear you. Is there a way to reach them so you can listen and understand one another?

Absolutely! A huge gap may lie between you and your teenagers today, but you can build a bridge to connect with them. It doesn't require any special materials or an engineering degree but it does require a unique perspective, some patience, and a compassionate attitude. If you are able to bring these qualities to your relationship with your teen then keep reading.

Before I start giving you the goods it's only fair that I share my story. After all, why should you listen to me unless you know a little about who I am? Well, it all began in Makkah, Saudi Arabia. My father was 20 years old when he had me and my biological mother was 28. She was from Thailand and my dad was from Syria. To say that my father wasn't prepared to have me might be an understatement. This caused a lot of tension between my parents and his family. Thus, they decided to get a divorce. I was only a few months old when she left. I don't remember my mother at all and I had moments throughout my teen years where I would feel alone, withdrawn and confused. Questions would race through my mind; "Why did she leave me? Was I not that important to her? Who am I?" Questions like these plagued my teenage years and everyone around me was oblivious to the pain that I felt.

To top that off, my father and I did not see eye to eye. Part of the reason was because he was about 10 inches taller than me. The other part was mainly due to our differing viewpoints on life, relationships and personal growth. He grew up in the Middle East with different values and beliefs. I grew up in the USA with a plethora of diversity and culture. What I saw as an opportunity to learn from others, he saw as a problem that could lead me in the wrong direction; which totally makes sense coming from his point of view. I mean I wasn't the perfect child growing up. I lied. I was a class clown. I ran away. I hung out with the wrong crowd. I performed poorly my freshman and sophomore years in high school until a teacher changed my outlook on life. I was also questioning things that made him feel uncomfortable about the way I viewed my life. He would do his best to help me see things right from wrong and good from bad, but his messages would never get through to me.

What was shocking was the fact that my friends would give similar advice as my dad would and I would listen to them in a heartbeat. This became a huge turning point! Why did I choose to listen to my friends over my father even though he had good intentions and they were practically saying the same exact things? This question led me on a journey to heal my relationship with my dad. I am happy to say that today my connection with him is unbreakable. We both have learned a lot from one another and will continue to do so. Sure we still have our disagreements but we also have a greater sense of respect and trust for one other. We have gone through countless arguments, abuse and tears to be where we are today. Whether you are a parent, teacher, or mental health professional this book will help you avoid the unnecessary pitfalls in getting through to your teen. My goal is to help you build a healthier relationship based on trust, respect, love and authenticity.

I structured this book in two parts. The first part is where we address the underlying problem. The second part is where we tackle the problem with heartfelt solutions. By the end of the book you will understand what teens (and in fact, all of us) seek. Why some teens seem intent on acting in challenging or defiant ways and what you as their parents, teachers and role models can do. In order to better understand young people and effectively connect with them we must first understand each other's point of view. Let's take a journey into the different worlds we live in.

# PART I

## THE
## UNDERLYING
## PROBLEM

# Mental World Wars

I AM CONVINCED THAT all wars, arguments and fights that have taken place throughout history and that will continue to take place in the world are a result of two simple, yet overlooked words: Perception and Perspective. Perception is how you **understand** the world around you (people, places, events, things, etc.). Perspective is how you **choose to look** at the world around you. *Perception can dramatically improve your perspective about your current reality.* In other words, understanding others can improve your outlook on life. The key word here is "understanding." Once we understand each other's worlds, we have a better foundation to build solid relationships.

You're probably asking, "Well, that's great Yahya, but what does this have to do with our teenagers?"

It has everything to do with our teenagers! The problem here is we don't really understand one another. The parent doesn't understand the teenager. The teacher doesn't understand the student. The teen doesn't understand either the parents or the teachers. Instead of listening to one another, we impose our beliefs by telling everyone what to do, assuming that we have the "right" perspective. There's a mental world war going on here! The real problem is that when we see others act outside of our perception, their behaviors are so foreign to us that we may think they are crazy, arrogant and immature. Therein lies part of the problem, because of this "perception issue" we automatically write them off. That's exactly how my father and I approached our relationship. I thought I was right and he thought he was right. I thought I was helping him and he thought he was helping me. Instead, we ended up arguing and becoming even more frustrated. I told my friends that he was the worst dad in the world and he would go and tell his friends that I was a disrespectful and confused troublemaker. *Have you ever judged a teenager or any other human being because you thought your outlook on life was better than theirs?* Of course you have! My favorite saying is, "Teenagers think that they know everything." If I had a nickel for every time someone said that to me, I would still have a nickel. Seriously though, many adults have said this exact statement and it is no wonder that teens don't listen to them. Their judgment stands in the way. The funny thing is we've all judged and have been judged before. There's no need to feel guilty though; as long as you are aware of it then you are already ahead of most people.

As my mentor Tony Robbins once said, "The moment we judge others, we lose all of our ability to impact and influence them in a positive direction." He is so right. How do we expect to help one another if we don't really understand where they are coming from? That is why in the next few chapters I will do my best to explain what really goes on in a parent's mind, a teacher's mind and a teenager's mind. Are you ready? Good, let's do this.

# The Parent's World

**B**EING A PARENT today is totally different than being a parent fifty years ago. With the advancement of technology, the collapse of our economy and divorces skyrocketing, it's safe to say that it's extremely challenging being a parent in today's world. Mothers and fathers have so many responsibilities it can practically seem overwhelming and impossible to maintain a healthy lifestyle. But here's the kicker, it's not what happens to you it's how you respond to your challenges that makes the difference. I know it's kind of a cliché but it's still a powerful statement. We all go through difficult times and sure the circumstances may be different for each person, but that doesn't really matter. What matters is how you deal with your problems. Allow me to share one of my personal stories with you.

When I was fourteen years old, I received an invitation to a house party. This was a huge party and almost every "popular" kid in school was going to be there. Of course, being a freshman and wanting to have the freedom to do what I wanted to do when I wanted to do it, I immediately decided to go to the party. So I put the invitation in the bottom drawer of my dresser right next to my bed. The part that I am embarrassed to tell you is that I didn't tell my father that I wanted to go or that I was going. Here's how I rationalized the whole scenario in my mind, "Well, I know baba (my father) is always uptight and he won't let me do anything, so I'll just tell him that I want to go to the movies. He'll buy that for sure." What you need to know is that the movie theatre was right across the street from our apartment. I thought this plan was clever. I told him that the movie started around 7:30 pm and it was a long movie. I can't recall the name of the movie that I gave him, but I can definitely recall the thrill and excitement of me going to that party.

It was around 12:30 in the morning when I decided to come back home. My heart was beating out of my chest. I thought, "What should I say when he asks me why I was late or how long the movie was?" I was so nervous. As I opened the door, I saw my dad eating dinner by himself. Across from him was an empty plate that he had placed the invitation to the party on. I slowly closed the door and I tried to apologize for being late. My father told me to shut my mouth and eat dinner. For the next 15 minutes there was an awkward silence. As I looked at him I figured he was up to something but didn't know what exactly. It was so quiet that you could hear a teardrop fall right onto the wooden floors. He didn't say a word. I didn't say a word. Talk about being embarrassed.

After I was done, I went directly to the bathroom to wash my hands and mouth. At this time, I was wearing my prescription glasses. As I was washing my hands my dad approached the bathroom door and politely asked me to take my glasses off. "You want me to take my glasses off?" I asked. "Yes," he replied, "now!" I took my glasses off and before I could even lay them down on the counter, "BOOOOOOMMMM!" I just got punched on the left side of my temple. I was out cold. As I woke up, I noticed that I was in the bathtub. I guess I fell in there after he hit me. I got up, took my glasses out of the sink and went directly to my room. On my way towards my room, which was located on the left side of the bathroom door, I notice my dad to my right sitting on the dinner table with his head down in his hands, crying as if someone just died in the family. It was around 2:30 am. It was the first time I have ever witnessed him crying. This was a surprise to me because he perceived crying as a weakness. My dad was a strong guy.

Instead of going to my room I approached him and placed my left hand on his shoulder. "It's okay," I said. It was hard for him to talk because he was crying so much. "I'm sorry Yahya. You don't understand how hard this is for me. I'm doing my best but nothing seems to work with you," he replied. As weird as this might sound, this was the first time I saw the human side of my father. I was used to the guy who was always telling me what to do and who had everything under control. In that moment, I didn't see him as the guy who had all the answers. I didn't see him as the evil man that I made him out to be. I saw him as an innocent child. I saw him as myself. That's when I realized the power that vulnerability possessed. My dad was just like every other human being on the face of the planet who made mistakes. We all make mistakes. We're not perfect. That's when I started to develop a new kind of respect and appreciation for him.

I share that story because it brings up a lot of interesting points. For one, parents don't have all the answers but sometimes they try and act like they do. I think this comes with a sense of protecting their children and their self-image. They want to make sure their children are in good hands and want to leave a good impression. This brings me to my next point; weakness. Sharing your flaws, mistakes, and weaknesses in a healthy way is probably one of the best things you can do as a parent. Obviously you don't want to throw a pity party, but you do want to share your humanness; especially **when the going gets tough**.

As Dr. Scott Wooding, Canada's leading authority on parenting teenagers, puts it, "Parents mistakenly assume that their teenagers don't want to talk with them. This assumption comes from the fact that teenagers are very poor at initiating conversation, especially on emotional issues. What parents don't realize is that there are a lot of hormonal changes that are going on throughout the teen years." Don't let the sudden silence discourage you. Just change your approach. The best way to do this is to spend some relaxing time with each other. Go to the mall, play games, or do some chores. I know this sounds simple but it's really overlooked. By the time parents come home, they're exhausted, stressed out and really don't have the time for leisure activities. Finding a way to manage this will give you huge rewards in the long run, not to mention it builds a closer relationship with your teen.

As a parent, the journey will always be challenging for you. Your children will have to go through the realities of dealing with peer pressure, drugs, alcohol, parties, bullying, unprotected sex, and performing well in school. You can't change the outside world with a click of a button. But you can change how you choose to respond to the outside world. That's all in your power. My advice is to stay calm in the face of these issues, especially when communicating with your teens. Showing that your angry, upset or hurt will guarantee you eliminating the chances for your teen to open up to you in the future. It's a game you need to learn if you want to have that connection with your teen. Once you get the mental game right, the physical and emotional will follow. I promise. My message to you parents is that it's okay to not have it all together. It's okay to make mistakes once in a while. Learn from them. Seek teen life coaches, relatives and therapists to help you get through to your teen. Sometimes it's better to have an unbiased person come into the equation.

# The Teacher's World

IF YOU ARE an educator or counselor, you are a teacher in my eyes. You teach students skills to mentally, physically and emotionally succeed in whatever they pursue. You help them to learn new and exciting information. You are a part of shaping their futures and I would like to acknowledge you for all the time, commitment and passion that you dedicate to helping your students. You play such a critical role in a student's life and in some cases maybe play a family figure to them. In this chapter we will briefly discuss what goes on in a teacher's world. I will also tell you how one teacher changed my life and the number one lesson to remember as a teacher.

Let's take a look at the world of a teacher from an outsider's perspective. Being a teacher today is no easy task. Teachers face more challenges now than they were facing a few years ago. For one, many teachers feel like they are underpaid. Obviously with the change in the economy and budget cuts that are occurring in many states, most of them are afraid of losing their jobs. It's tough to help students when you are constantly worried about your own security. In addition, the rise of bullying, peer pressure, drugs, alcohol, sexting and every other issue deemed imaginable is getting in the way of the teacher really providing their students with the best educational environment. Not only do they have to educate their students but they also have to deal with other baggage that's not being addressed properly outside of the schools. Sometimes when teachers try to speak to their student's parents, they feel as if their parents don't even care as much as they should. That really hurts a teacher's drive because they feel like no one cares about the work that they are putting in, other than themselves. Have you ever felt like no one cared about your time and efforts? I've definitely felt that way before.

Throughout my life as a student, I've met teachers who really didn't care about their roles as educators. Maybe it was because there wasn't a sense of support involved. For instance, parents wouldn't team up with teachers to really help their children succeed. Or maybe they became teachers because it was the "easiest" thing to do in that moment in their lives. Side note: If this is you, I highly suggest you watch the movie, *Freedom Writers.* It's such an inspirational movie and it will motivate you to give your best to your students. Okay, back on track. I've also met teachers who were so sincere and passionate about helping their students succeed, that they would do it whether or not there was a salary involved. Don't get me wrong, making money is very, very important, especially when you have bills, a family and other expenses that must be taken care of, but that shouldn't be the main reason why a person becomes a teacher. So rather than wasting your time with what you already know, I'll share my own experience with a teacher who was very passionate about her work. Let it be noted that I hated this woman but in the end she changed my perspective on life and education.

It was the beginning of my sophomore year in the fall of 2003. Let it also be known that I hated English class. Critical thinking is a teenager's worst nightmare! That's why I have a bunch of contractions and grammatical errors in my writing. I just go with the flow. Mind you, at this time I never studied or put any effort in my schoolwork. We had to take an English test that was written by our English teacher Ms. Lindenbaum. She was this petite, blond woman that had this monotone voice that would put an alarm clock to sleep. If you're reading this Ms. Lindenbaum, don't take it personally. You're really awesome.

As I was taking the test, the voice in my head was like, "This is a waste of my time." So I just wrote paragraphs that made no sense whatsoever. I put no effort into the test at all. I was the first one done in my class, which gave me a sense of accomplishment. Two days later, I get the test back. I received an "F" circled in red ink. Underneath the circle was the comment, "Yahya, you are wasting your time and potential by not giving your best. It's so sad." I don't know what had gotten into me. Maybe it was the last three words that caused me to black out and make a huge fuss. I literally flipped out. I started cursing at her using words that I did not even think were capable coming from my mouth. I ripped the paper in half and stood up. She looked at me with a smile and in a calm voice she asked, "Yahya, would you please speak to me out in the hallway?" I walked outside knowing that I dug myself into a huge hole. I was so angry but it felt so good. I was in control. Looking back at it now, I chose to look bad rather than be embarrassed. Ms. Lindenbaum came out of the classroom and shut the door behind her.

**Ms. Lindenbaum:** "Yahya, I'm not going to send you to the principal's office or give you detention."

*I was in shock that she said that because I was expecting the worst from her.*

**Ms. Lindenbaum:** "You know why?"

**Me:** Why?

**Ms. Lindenbaum:** "Because we all fail Yahya. We all get angry and lose control of our emotions too."

**Me:** "Whatever."

**Ms. Lindenbaum:** "I'm serious. Failure doesn't define who you are and you probably got angry because you were seeking attention to make yourself feel better. You can use that attention to your advantage Yahya. You are a likable guy. A lot of people look up to you. You are funny, enthusiastic and when you're acting silly, your classmates actually listen to you."

*At this moment, I was flattered by what she said and embarrassed by my behavior.*

**Ms. Lindenbaum:** "Let's put this incident behind us. I will give you an opportunity to retake the test but it will be with different questions and passages. Will you accept that opportunity?"

**Me:** "Yea, sure . . . . . and I'm sorry."

**Ms. Lindenbaum:**   (with a smile) "No need to be sorry. Just promise me that you will give it your best. You deserve it."

**Me:**   "Okay. I promise."

I'll admit, that moment was a very unique, awkward and a life-changing moment for me. I mean, who does that? Would you do something like that if a student of yours started acting out and threatened you? But she somehow managed to see the best in me without judging. Two days later I ended up getting a B+ on that test. Fast forward to my senior year of high school, I had a 3.6 GPA. I received honor roll in each marking period. Now, I am not expecting you to do that with your students. I just wanted to share that story because she did three things that dramatically shifted my outlook on, not only life, but also more importantly myself.

1. **She remained calm.** *Ms. Lindenbaum didn't lose her composure, which totally shocked me. That's definitely one way of getting my attention.*

2. **She related to me.** *She didn't just point out all the things I did wrong. I was very well aware of what I did but she somehow managed to make me feel safe around her.*

3. **She saw my potential.** *This is probably why I respect her so much. She was able to rise above her fear, judgment and status and fully see who I was capable of becoming. After all, I deserved to give everything my best.*

What is the number one lesson that we can learn from Ms. Lindenbaum? That who you are as a person is more important than what you say and what you do. You see, she could've said a number of things to me that day but none of it would have impacted me in a positive way. She could have changed my grade immediately or sent me to detention but it still wouldn't have taught me a lesson. On that day I was able to see a genuine person who cared. She was more than just a teacher; she was a human being. She put her ego aside for just a moment to fully address my insecurities and she did so with dignity, compassion and strength. I will always remember her as the teacher who taught me a life lesson. So I invite you to surround yourself with amazing teachers, coaches, speakers and counselors who know how to get through to students. Ask them questions. We all need positive role models. If you haven't done so yet, pretty soon it will be you who will have positively impacted a student's life. Remember, when it comes to students and life in general, the impact that you make isn't necessarily from what you talk about and what you do, but it's from who you are as a human.

# The Teenager's World

I DON'T THINK WE give teenagers as much credit as they deserve. Out of all worlds, the teenager's world has to be the most confusing, challenging and risky one of all. Do you remember what it was like being a teenager? I know times have changed but I bet the feelings, patterns and behaviors were probably the same in each generation. I can't prove that assumption but I can attempt to understand what in the world is going on through a teenager's mind. Of course, what I say in this chapter doesn't hold true for all the teenagers in the entire world, but a general understanding will suffice for now. In this chapter we will identify the three phases of life and how you come into the picture.

According to Stephen Covey, author of *The 7 Habits of Highly Effective People*, we all go through three distinct phases of life. The first phase is dependence, which is approximately between the ages of zero and eleven years old. Imagine you're raising your little newborn baby and watching them grow up faster than you can say "Yahya!" They transition from being an infant to a toddler to a pre-school kid to a school-kid and it all happens way to quick! During the dependent phase, parents become so attached to their little babies that when puberty comes along it's like a slap in their face. This is the time when parents need to switch their mindset. They need to understand that their kids are on a journey to become men and women and that it's okay to let them fail. Don't be afraid to let them fail. Don't waste your energy trying to cover up their failures. Allow them to learn from their failures and help them go on to the next challenge. It's OK to fail. If people aren't failing, they're not growing.

Next comes the phase of independence, which is approximately between the ages of eleven and seventeen. This is when a teenager becomes curious. Risk-taking is at an all-time high during these years. As Laurence Steinberg, a developmental psychologist specializing in adolescence at Temple University, points out, even 14— to 17-year-olds—the biggest risk takers—use the same basic cognitive strategies that adults do, and they usually reason their way through problems just as well as adults.

Contrary to popular belief, they also fully recognize they're mortal. And, like adults, says Steinberg, "teens actually overestimate risk." If this is the case, then why do the majority of teenagers make such hasty and risky decisions? The answer is simple. They value immediate rewards more than long-term negative consequences.

In addition to their risky behaviors, these are the times that define who they are and who they're capable of becoming. They also start to question and defy authority. But due to lack of mentorship, guidance and emotional support, teenagers can be easily manipulated. Thus they start hanging around with crowds that they can relate to but may not have their best interests in mind. Let's not forget that their hormones are raging throughout their physiology and they start seeing adults as people who just don't get what they're going through. Sometimes they're right. That's why they value their friends so much. Not only can they relate to them but they also give them something to look forward to in the future. Connection is everything for a teenager.

Now pay attention because this is important. Mel Levine, one of the leading experts on learning disabilities, defined adolescence in one sentence. He said, "Adolescence is a 24 hour a day, 7 day a week, 365 day a year battle to not be embarrassed." What that means is that their greatest fear is that of being humiliated by others. Dr. Rick Lavoie, author of the *Motivation Breakthrough,* stated that at any given moment, any teenager would prefer to be viewed as a bad kid then a dumb kid. If you put them in a position to choose between looking bad or dumb, 90% of the time they will choose to be bad. Key thing to take away is that teenagers do not need another person to tell them that what they did was wrong, especially in front of others. This is a subtle but powerful shift in understanding.

Finally comes the phase of interdependence, which is approximately between the ages of eighteen until death. Please don't confuse interdependence with codependence. There is a huge difference. Interdependence involves a person taking responsibility for their feelings, desires and actions. Codependence involves a person not taking responsibility for their feelings, desires and actions and expecting others to fulfill their needs for them at a moment's call. Interdependence is when the teenager becomes an adult and is interacting with others in a healthy manner. Their relationships within the family, at work and most importantly, with themselves, are thriving.

These phases are very important to understand because it will give you a glimpse through the teenager's mind. Out of these three phases, which one do you think is the most difficult? Yup! You guessed correctly, it's without a doubt the phase of independence. This can seem problematic at first but if we just shift our perspective by a tiny hair, we'll notice that teenagers are highly adaptable ninja turtles! According to B. J. Casey, a neuroscientist at Weill Cornell Medical College who has spent nearly a decade applying brain and genetic studies to our understanding of adolescence, he says, "We're so used to seeing adolescence as a problem. But the more we learn about what really makes this period unique, the more adolescence starts to seem like a highly functional, even adaptive period." The way that I interpret what Dr. Casey states is that teenagers can take a worst-case scenario and turn it into a success story. That's amazing! All they need is a master Splinter to guide them throughout the process. That's it!

Take me for example. A high school kid mugged me at the age of 11 on the street. Fast forward 4 years later and I became a 2 time National Jr. Olympic Champion in Taekwondo with ten gold medals, three silver medals and one bronze medal while attaining my first-degree black belt. I became a success because my father told me that I could either complain about what happened to me or I could start learning how to defend myself to make sure this wouldn't happen in the future. And so I decided to create my future. The choice was left up to me. I had my independence but I also had the guidance of my father in that moment. Also, remember when I failed my English test? What happened? I got an F and then turned it into a B+, which inspired me to take my freshman year GPA of 2.1 up to my senior year GPA of 3.6. I became a success because I had a great teacher help change my perspective. Let's not forget about the pain and confusion that I had about my biological mother leaving and my relationship with my father turning into a mess. These experiences have become the source of inspiration for helping parents, teachers and teenagers all over the world.

Sure, there are a lot of hormonal changes occurring during the adolescent years that can drive you crazy. But this is a good sign because that means that they will be going through mood swings, risk-taking adventures and misbehaviors TEMPORARILY. Your job is to make sure you do your best to guide them throughout their formative years without being pushy. What I am saying is that they can't do this without you. They need you more than ever even though their hormones might say otherwise. It is my mission to make sure you effectively connect with them in the best way possible. That's why in part two, you will discover a simple yet powerful framework, formula and connection strategy that will inspire you towards becoming the master Splinter in their lives. Do you have a better understanding now than you did before? Good. I told you it was all a matter of perspective.

# PART II

## THE COMPASSIONATE SOLUTION

# The Coach's World

WOULD YOU MIND doing me a quick favor? When it comes to communicating to teenagers, forget about what you believe to be right or wrong for just a moment. Release all the judgments and stereotypes that you might have about yourself and about them. Since we want to be able to really get through to teens, we need to start from scratch. This might seem contradictory to what you're used to but I need you to trust me here. In this chapter we will focus on shifting your perspective from a parent and teacher point of view into a coach's point of view. This subtle shift is paramount to your success as a role model and you'll see why in just a second.

What do Michael Jordan, Oprah, Anthony Robbins, Nelson Mandela and Serena Williams all have in common? Besides the fact that they all have the letter "a" in their names; they also had the best coaches to take them from where they were to where they wanted to be. What's interesting to point out here is that these individuals are top-notch people who don't really need any help, coming from our point of view, but they still desire the support and direction to perform at their best. Why? I have no idea but the fact still remains that they all performed at their highest level and were able to change the course of history in sports, politics, and our overall quality of life.

A great coach is one who sets high standards, believes in a person's capabilities and accepts failure as part of the process towards success. They have developed patience because they understand that it takes time to do extremely well. They remind others to give their best. They encourage their students to take full responsibility for their thoughts, words and actions. At the same time they understand that their students will make a few mistakes here and there and that's okay. As long as they can learn from their mistakes they are moving in a positive direction. They challenge their students to think outside of themselves. They empower others to uncover what's possible for their lives. In short, great coaches are strategists who have mastered the art of turning self-imposed limiting beliefs into self-fulfilling success stories.

Right now, I'm not speaking to the parent or teacher that you already are. I'm speaking to the courageous coach that is already within you. And as a coach, you must understand that teenagers all over the world need your guidance. They are our future world-class athletes, leaders, professionals, parents, philanthropists, artists and musicians in the making. They all have the capacity to be great and they need you to step up. They don't need a friend. They don't need a person telling them what to do or what is right or wrong. They need you to believe in them, guide them and show them that they are greater than what they've allowed themselves to believe. You are the coach that they have been waiting for. Once they see you shift into this mindset, they will have no idea what hit them. They will listen to you with open hearts and welcoming minds. They will respect you like you wouldn't believe because you took the time to acknowledge their greatness and respect them. Finally, they will love and appreciate you unconditionally because you've helped them succeed throughout their phase of independence; the most confusing, challenging and vulnerable phase in their lives.

With that said, let's begin by sharing the framework that I use to understand what motivates a teenager to do the things they do. By the way, welcome to the coach's world.

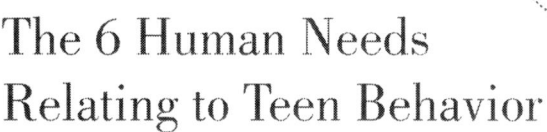

# The 6 Human Needs
# Relating to Teen Behavior

Y OU MIGHT BE wondering why I titled this book *Beyond Motivation!* Well besides the fact that I thought it was an awesome title, the name of the book was inspired by a conversation I had with a principal at a high school I recently spoke in. I asked him, "What do you think is the #1 problem that most of your students face?" He quickly replied, "Students aren't that motivated these days. There are so many issues that are distracting them from receiving a great education; bullying, peer pressure, drug and alcohol abuse, poor examples of leadership, to name a few. That's why we brought you in, so you can motivate them." While his response was well intentioned, the truth is I can't motivate a person. I can only put things into perspective for them and in order to do that, I would need to go beyond the ordinary concept of motivation. So let's breakdown the framework to understand why teenagers are motivated to do the things they do.

We are probably most familiar to the concepts of human needs psychology through legendary psychologist, Abraham Maslow and his Hierarchy of Needs pyramid. In short, he stated that we all have basic needs that must be met before we could move on to self-actualization. Well, what are our basic needs? We need food to eat and water to drink. We need shelter, enough money to get by, and medicine. We will do what we have to do in order to make sure these needs are being met. In other words, we are motivated to do what we have to do to make sure our needs are met. In Dr. Rick Lavoie's book, *Motivation Breakthrough,* he states that *all human behavior is motivated.* If this is true, that would mean that teenagers are motivated to bully, to do drugs and alcohol, to behave the way they do because those actions are meeting certain needs for them. If our mental, physical and emotional needs are not met in healthy, beneficial ways, then we find unproductive and sometimes dangerous ways to satisfy thcm. According to behavioral change expert Anthony Robbins, as well as renowned psychotherapist Cloe Madanes, all human behavior can be boiled down in to the following six human needs. This is the framework I use to understand what motivates a teenager.

## THE FRAMEWORK

1. **Certainty**—the need to experience pleasure without pain. *Keywords are: safety, stability, comfort, schedule, routine, structure, plan and commitment*

2. **Variety**—the need for change and stimulation. *Keywords are: fun, excitement, adventure, different, and new.*

3. **Significance**—the need to feel important and valuable. *Keywords are: worthy, best, pride, power, top, and control.*

4. **Love/Connection**—the need to be cared for and cared about. *Keywords are: friends, family, and peers.*

5. **Growth**—the need to become better and to improve our skills. *Keywords: learn, achieve, read, practice, and challenge.*

6. **Contribution**—the need to give beyond one's self. Keywords: *share, give, volunteer, help, and teach.*

## 1) CERTAINTY

Routines let us feel some control over the world. Wake up, shower, get dressed, have a cup of coffee (or four), go to work. We think routines keep life running smoothly, and we can be productive. A sense of certainty brings us comfort that we know what is going to happen. Lack of certainty can be distracting and frightening.

## 2) VARIETY

On the other hand, no one wants every single day to be identical to the next. People need variety; that's why they try new dishes at restaurants, talk to new people, and ride roller coasters. While certainty makes us feel comfortable and secure, variety makes us feel vibrant and alive. Variety is the spice of life.

## 3) SIGNIFICANCE

Everyone needs to feel that he or she has value. We need to feel that we make a difference and that the world would be a different—and worse—place without us. People are driven by significance because it provides them a sense of validation and accomplishment.

## 4) LOVE AND CONNECTION

This can come in all forms. It can be romantic love, searching for "The One." It can be the affection of a child, of a pet, of our friends. It can be finding a team or club with like-minded people. It can be the genuine care of a teacher or parent. Love and connection keep us from feeling alone.

## 5) GROWTH

Sure, most of us would like to be a couple of inches taller, but this isn't what we mean by "growth." Growth refers to our need to challenge ourselves and learn new things. Without this, we would have no skills and we would depend on others to take care of us.

## 6) CONTRIBUTION

We all need to give back to the world. This can refer to volunteering and doing charity work, but it doesn't have to. Throwing a party, for example, impacts many people beyond the host, and is also a form of contribution.

While everyone has all six needs, each individual fulfills those needs differently. Some people crave certainty, and cling to their routines, while others need variety, and will always try new things. Some have such a need for significance that they will do anything to be noticed, while others feel the need to contribute so strongly that they throw themselves into a life of charity work.

As we grow up, we learn how to satisfy our needs. Most of the time, we satisfy them in healthy ways. But some people, if they know no other options, will use counterproductive or destructive means to meet their needs.

*Bottom line, every need must be met, and will be met in healthy or unhealthy ways.* Here are a couple of examples:

- *To meet the need for variety, someone may audition for a school play, or may go skiing for the first time. These are healthy ways of meeting that need. Some people, however, drink heavily or try drugs as a way of experiencing new states of mind. These are obviously unhealthy ways to meet the need.*

- *To feel significant, people can run for political office, can publish a piece of writing or display a work of art, or can prepare dinner for their families. Acting rudely or disruptively and using violence, however, are negative ways to meet the need for significance.*

- *Contributing is often a benevolent thing. You can teach children, become a volunteer coach, or work with a charity to give back to the world. Sometimes, however, people become addicted to contributing to the point where they neglect their own well-being. Do you know someone like this?*

*Take a few moments and think about how the six human needs apply to you. See if you can come up with several healthy and unhealthy ways to meet them.*

The six human needs have EVERYTHING to do with behavior—good or bad, child, teen, or adult. Look, if teens can meet their needs at a high level, they will, but many of them are not equipped with the life skills to make the right choices. *Meeting our emotional needs isn't something we are born with; it's an acquired skill.* So, if your teen exhibits challenging behavior, it can only be a result of five simple observations.

1. Teenagers haven't learned how to meet their needs in productive ways.

2. Parents, teachers and friends aren't really helping them fulfill their needs.

3. Parents, teachers and friends might not know how to address their teen's needs effectively.

4. The environment they're surrounded in isn't helping them fulfill their needs

5. All of the above.

Let's look at an example.

Q: Mark is an average student who usually passes his exams, but rarely performs well on them. He doesn't participate in extra—curricular activities or sports. He is also the third of four boys in his family, and both of his older brothers are academically and athletically gifted. Mark rarely answers questions in class, but will interrupt other students to tell outrageous and startling stories that are unrelated to class activities. His teacher calls his parents, saying that Mark has an attitude problem and likes to hog attention. Is the teacher's assessment correct?

A: While the teacher's frustration is certainly justified, and it is true that Mark seeks attention, he is not just a kid with a bad attitude. One of his emotional needs is not being met, probably the need for significance. Mark feels unimportant and unnoticed because of his weak academic, athletic, and social skills. Since he has not yet learned how to make a positive impact on his environment, he makes himself noticed the only way he knows how— interrupt and shock his classmates.

## GREAT. BUT WHAT CAN I DO ABOUT IT?

If you needed to fix a clogged drain but didn't know how, what would you do? If you were reading a recipe and didn't know how to pan sear something, what would you do? You would *learn the skill.* If your child or student is showing troubling behavior what do you do? Help them *learn the skill.*

This happens in two steps. First, you need to identify which emotional need (or needs) is being met with the behavior. In the example of Mark above, it was the need for significance. Secondly, the teen must be guided to look at the behavior and **re-evaluate** it to find a healthier solution.

Let's look at Mark again. What might be some better ways to meet the need for significance? If he has a talent that can be shared (Art, Music, Theater), he could be encouraged to explore that (participate in school art galleries, start a band, try making positive contributions in class or at home ("Thank you, Mark, for taking out the trash." "That's a great comment, Mark. You're really on-target today!") These will help Mark learn to meet his need for significance in positive ways, and he will no longer need to resort to disruptive behavior.

Remember, these solutions are not prescriptive. Mark's parent cannot tell him to try out for a play and expect an immediate reversal of his behavior. Learning to meet our emotional needs in new ways can be a lengthy and challenging process that would require self-awareness, awareness of others, and patience.

"But I've tried all that Yahya. I've done everything! Why is it so hard for them to change their behavior?"

It is important to stop and realize that teenagers are not the only ones meeting emotional needs in unhealthy ways. We do this, too. The "risky behavior" in teens become "bad habits" in our daily lives. This book isn't about how to "fix" teenagers, nor is it about gaining control over them; it is about how to better understand them, better understand ourselves, and build better relationships.

With that in mind, why is it so hard to change a negative behavior? Well, it's much easier to recognize a negative behavior in someone else than in ourselves. We become used to our negative choices, and after long enough, they become more than just actions. They become part of our very identity! Identifying ourselves with our problems is a collaborative process; we do it to ourselves, and people do it to us, as well.

For example, if Natalie drives recklessly, climbs fences, and experiments with drugs, it is easy to label her as a "risk-taker" or a "daredevil." After long enough, people won't see Natalie's behavior as behavior; they will see it as part of who she is. Eventually, she will identify herself by those behaviors, and then changing the behavior becomes much more difficult. Rather than saying Natalie IS a risk-taker, say she is BEHAVING in dangerous ways. That way, the behavior stays separate from the individual, and it is much easier to fix.

"But a bad home situation, a dysfunctional relationship, or a traumatic event can change someone's personality. What if the teen's behavior is someone else's fault?"

Life rarely runs smoothly. Everyone experiences setbacks and trauma, and their importance should not be overlooked. As role models, we must be sensitive to the underlying causes of human behavior. A student acting out in class may be suffering from a problem the teacher has no idea about. A suddenly moody child may be dealing with challenges the parent is unaware of. Often, these circumstances are something the child can do nothing about.

But guess what? *Everyone* has setbacks and trauma. What sets those who can go on to lead emotionally, mentally and physically healthy lives from those stuck in patterns of destructive thought and behavior? *Response.* That's it! In this life, we will all find and lose jobs, fall in love and have hearts broken, make friends and be betrayed. This is inevitable. How we respond to these events, however, is our choice and that's what we need to teach adolescents.

But for some reason, some of us might not think of it that way. We have been conditioned from birth to think that certain actions must be followed by certain emotional reactions. When someone dumps you, you get mad at them. When your boss fires you, he's a jerk . If you're cut from the team, the coach plays favorites. Sometimes, the trauma is more severe, and we carry it with us for years. Abuse, infidelity, bullying, these things can affect our behavior for our entire lives—but only if we let them. *We cannot control what happens to us, but we can control how we respond.* We can choose to let our problems define us, or we can choose to use them and grow.

The message here isn't to just keep on smiling, pretending bad things never happen. This approach isn't about denial; it's about responsibility. Let's break that word down. Response/ability. Being responsible is having the ability to CHOOSE your response to events in positive ways. What we must do—and what we must teach our children—is learn this. This knowledge isn't something we're born with. It is something that must be taught and practiced.

This is where you, as parents and educators, can help. When we can get past the labeling and identifying people with their problems (Mark is an attention hog, Natalie is a trouble maker), we can teach our children and students to respond to events in positive ways. When Mark feels frustrated that no one pays attention to him, acknowledge those feelings and help him find positive ways to gain attention. When Natalie gets in trouble for risky behavior, acknowledge her need for variety and her adventurous spirit, and then work with her to find adventures that are opportunities to grow and learn. And remember— learning the ability to respond positively is a skill. It takes patience, practice, and dedication to master it. But once you've set your sights in the right direction—identifying emotional needs that are being met in negative ways, and then re-evaluating responses—you and the teen in your life will be on the path to a healthy, meaningful relationship.

I know this chapter was dramatically longer than the rest but it's because this framework is the key to getting to the root cause of a teenager's disconnected behavior. When you fully understand the six human needs and start playing with the idea that teenagers are always motivated, you will move into the perspective that they are not a problem but an opportunity. Now that we have the understanding of the framework involved in understanding what motivates teens to do what they do, it's time to reveal the formula that ALWAYS leads to trust, appreciation and service when it comes to communicating with them.

# The Secret 2 Part Formula for Teen Life Transformation

JUST FOR THE sake of simplicity, when I refer to the term "relationship", I mean every single person who we can relate to. This can stand for friends, family members, coworkers, students as well as teenagers.

Now, we've all heard that communication is the backbone of all successful relationships. If we were to take this assumption and apply it into our daily lives, we'd realize that communication isn't really the only ingredient needed to make sure a relationship thrives. I mean almost anyone can open their mouths and say what's on their mind. We hear this every day. "Don't do this. Don't do that. Didn't I tell you that you . . . ?" You see, communication works to a certain degree but it's the first step guaranteeing your way to create an amazing bond with your teen.

Without further ado, I present to you my *secret 2 part formula* for relationship success. I dare you to apply this formula into any social interaction and watch what happens.

## MY SECRET 2 PART FORMULA

1.  Communication + Compassion= Connection

2.  Contribution+ Community= Commitment

Allow me to break this formula down for you. When you communicate compassionately to a teenager, you open up the opportunity to connect with them. Once you get the connection, the ball is in your court. You can then give them any advice you believe will contribute to their mental, physical and emotional success. Instead of them seeing you as enemies, now they see you as respectful allies. Once they see the value that you contributed to them, they will be in the position to be greater role models who will effectively impact and inspire the people around them. All this will result in a more positive, healthy and successful community which will lead them to a life of commitment to their words, to their actions and to the promises they keep with the people they have not only communicated to, but connected to as well. Sure it was a mouthful but read it again.

In other words, you need to communicate compassionately so you can connect. When you connect then you can correct them. This will guide them into a state of contributing to a greater sense of community that will ultimately lead them into a life filled with commitment.

When I coach parents, teachers and teenagers to fully connect to each other, I always remind them that it takes time and awareness to make this work. So many people, including myself at times, get the formula all mixed up. As role models, we do our best to make sure we guide teens towards the "right" direction so they can make positive choices and stay out of trouble. It is our nature to want to *contribute* to them. However, once we feel that we have something that will help them, we do our best to *communicate* with them and expect them to *commit* to the promises of change so they can move towards a positive direction, but to no success.

For instance, you might think that it's really important for your teen to be on top of their schoolwork so that they can get a better education in the near future. You talk to them and tell them why you think it's so important for them to focus on their schoolwork and get a better education and they nod their heads in haste hoping to end the conversation immediately. They reply with the dreaded "I know. I know this already." You might even try to motivate and reward them with some really cool incentives. You want them to commit to the change that you had in mind for them because you absolutely know that it will benefit them, but one month later, there is minimal progress if any at all. Why does this happen? It's because the formula wasn't applied in the right sequence.

Instead of immediately communicating with them about what you think is right, see if you can understand what they might be going through. Be loving and firm. Show them that you care about them and you won't expect anything less from them because you know who they are capable of becoming and what they are capable of giving. Ask them questions about topics that they can relate to. Use what works and throw out what doesn't. If you feel as if you've tried everything but nothing is working, schedule a coaching session with me to see how I can help you and your teen build a better relationship. The key thing to understand is that you need to establish a connection before you can get a commitment from them. If you aren't doing that, you are setting yourself up for disaster.

Maybe you don't agree with my approach. You might feel as if it's not your job to connect with them and figure out what motivates them. I've had parents and teachers come up to me and say, "Yahya, I'm not here to play detective and build a relationship with them. I am their teacher/ parent and they're supposed to do what is told. If they don't listen, that's not my responsibility, it's theirs. They will suffer with the consequences and learn the hard way. I don't want to be their friends; I'm an authority figure for them." I agree with the last part. Teens need a role model that they can learn from and look up to; they don't need you to be the go to person to share all their little secrets. They want to feel safe around you and you can provide them that certainty. But the rest just seems way over the top. It sounds like those individuals have a "power" issue and they are trying to meet their need for significance by controlling their teen's behavior. Josh Shipp, a good friend of mine who is also a teen behavior expert, states that you can't just tell them what to do; you have to show them too. Show AND tell is the name of the game, not show OR tell. He is absolutely correct.

Here are my two cents, if what you are doing is working and your relationship with your teen is based on trust, respect, authenticity and appreciation, then keep doing what you're doing. However, if your relationship is based on misunderstanding, resentment, aggression, or fear, then maybe it's time for a "connection tune-up." In the following chapter, I will share my *Ultimate Connection Process*, so you not only walk away with the understanding of what's blocking your ability to get through to teens effectively, but you walk away with the tools to really take your *connection game* to the next level.

PART

II

# The Ultimate
# Connection Process

*"The better your connection with your child, the more
they want to please you."*
—Dr. Laura Markham, Parenting Expert

FINALLY, THIS IS what we've been waiting for.
Now that we've got the framework and formula
stored into our subconscious minds, it's time to uncover
the simple, straightforward and strategic 7 step process
to make sure you can connect with your teens effectively,
empathetically and efficiently. First, I would recommend
that you use these strategies when you are alone with
your teen or student. Why? Because a teenager's #1 fear
is the fear of being humiliated. If they are in front of
others or if you are extremely strict with them, they will
lie to you because their social lives are dependent on
it. If you can't provide them with a safe environment,

this process will fall apart. I challenge you to approach them with a non-judgmental mindset. Observe their body language and understand that they want to open up to you but they just don't know how yet. Remember, you're here because you want to build a relationship based on trust, authenticity and appreciation. Let go of the need to "fix" them; accept them for who they are and separate their behavior from their identity. It's time to breakthrough.

## 7 Strategies To Breakthrough To Teens

### 1) *Begin with your Beliefs*

A. *These might seem like redundant questions, but they're very important ones.*

1. What is your motive?

2. Do you want to change teenagers because they're foolish or do you want to help them because they deserve caring guidance?

3. Do you believe you have the best interest in mind for your teenager or student?

4. Do you think the specific teen that you are reaching out to is a troublemaker, brat, or some other negative word that I won't express in this book?

5. Do you see yourself as a role model who can positively impact their lives for the better?

6. Why do teenagers need to listen to you?

B. *Whether you're a teacher, parent, youth worker or friend, you must value your ability to help others in order for them to value your time, knowledge and experience.*

C. *As the old saying goes, "You better check yourself before you wreck yourself." If you don't check your beliefs and intentions about why you want to help a teenager, you might wreck the whole conversation before it begins.*

*D. EXAMPLE: Before engaging in a serious conversation with your teen, stop for a moment and ask yourself the previous questions. See if the answers to those questions move in the direction of manipulation or inspiration. Inspiration is what you are looking for. All great role models inspire. Believe in your ability to inspire.*

## 2) Break the Barrier

A. *Vulnerability always wins.*

1. No one wants to hear about your successes. Everyone wants to hear about your mistakes. Be authentic. Don't try to be someone you're not (i.e. perfect).

2. If you made a mistake, own up to it and promise that you'll do a better job next time. Then, do your best to keep your word. That's how you gain respect.

B. *Share your uniqueness.*

1. Be creative! Do you sing, dance, paint or do something different? Are you funny or goofy? Share it with them. Teens can relate to being different. It's the story of their lives. That's how you break the ice.

C. *EXAMPLE: If you notice that your teen isn't interested in talking to you, rather than taking it personally, show/tell them something that immediately catches them off guard. You want to make sure they drop their guards. For instance, I beat box (making "cool" sounds with my mouth that sounds like music). They think that's different and cool. You don't have to beat box, but you do have to do something that's unexpected. Think outside the box here.*

### 3) Bridge the Gap

A. *Get over yourself!*

1. Get over yourself so you can understand them. No play on words here. Understand their world; see their perspective and listen.

Even if you believe that what they're doing is COMPLETELY wrong, at least you took the time to acknowledge them.

2. Don't be so quick to judge. Pay attention to their problems and needs regardless of how silly it may sound.

B. *ALWAYS REMEMBER: The moment you judge a person, you lose all of your ability to influence, inspire and impact them towards a positive direction.*

C. *EXAMPLE: Let's say that your son, daughter or student is involved in drugs, alcohol, bullying, sex or some other negative behavior. The normal response is to freak out and tell them that what they're doing is wrong and unacceptable. Although this is true, you need to understand why they are choosing to use those vehicles to meet their needs. Once you figure out the why, then you can address the what, when, where, who and how. Getting to the root of the problem is way more effective than scaring them for the temporary moment.*

## 4) Build the Bond

A. *Admire them for their courage.*

    1. Give them praise and commend them on their level of honesty and humility.

B. *Connect*

    1. Share a moment in your lifetime where you can relate to their feelings or have done something similar to what they've done.

C. *Guide them.*

    1. Once you connect to them emotionally, then you can empower and educate them by stating the facts and any concerns or information you might have for them.

2. Allow them to experience their independence and let them fail a few times. They are looking for someone to guide them, not for someone to breathe down their necks over every decision they make.

D. *EXAMPLE: Let's say your teen or student doesn't want to do their homework. Follow the previous steps and then share a personal story when you dreaded doing your homework. Get very specific. Express what you felt and what was going through your mind. Once you see them engaged, then you can introduce your lesson, facts or concerns. Reassure them that they will make the best decision possible.*

## 5) *Boost the Benefits*

A. *Grow your relationship over time.*

1. Now that you have built the foundation you can enjoy all the positive aspects of your relationship with them.

2.  Benefits include but are not limited to: laughing joyously, living fully, learning constantly, loving generously, sharing openly, speaking honestly and more.

**B.**  *Example: After you have built rapport with them and they know that you care, you will have many opportunities to be there for each other. Instead of talking about problems all the time, maybe you can talk about things that put a smile on your face (i.e. Hilarious Youtube video: "Charlie Bit My Finger", Awesome Youtube video: "Dubstep Dance").*

## 6) *Balance Each other*

A.  *Noise, Static and Confusion.*

1.  There will be times when your connection is out of sync. After all that you did, they went back to their old patterns and behaviors. Don't worry, this is normal. Everyone goes through a lot throughout the day. The key is to make sure you are balancing each other out.

2. In order for the relationship to stay centered, you need to always make sure you are both on the same wave length. Follow up, let them know you care and have their best interest at heart. Rinse & Repeat.

B. *EXAMPLE: In the pH scale you have two extremes; acid (0) and alkaline (14). To maintain balance you always want to be approximately in the middle; neutral (7-7.4). In the Ultimate Connection Strategy you also have two extremes; uninvolved and over involved. To maintain balance you always want to be approximately in the middle: interested in their personal well-being. (Notice I didn't say, frustrated with their lack of progress or unacceptable attitude). Know that everyone moves from positive intent and sometimes we just get knocked off of balance.*

## 7) *Broaden Your Breakthrough*

A. *Apply the Ultimate Connection Process with anyone.*

1. Teenagers will probably be the most challenging individuals you'll ever talk to/ establish a connection with. Being able to breakthrough to them is a skill that needs to be constantly developed, but once you get the basics down you can take these skills in any other area of your life. Whether it's in your career, family life or just a new person who might have a specific problem, being able to breakthrough to them is a skill you do want to have.

2. The 7 Step process is universal and powerful. Master them and you will have almost everyone trusting, respecting and admiring you as a positive role model. Don't be surprised if other parents, teachers, mental health professionals and teenagers start coming up to you for advice.

B. *EXAMPLE: After applying the Ultimate Connection Strategy and using the tips and techniques that you already know, you were able to turn a troubled and disconnected teen into an amazing and inspiring role model. Now teachers, parents and others are asking, "What in the world did you do?" Not only will you tell them what you've been doing, but you'll also show them how you got involved in learning the Ultimate Connection Strategy. This will provide you with a circle of individuals who you know you can trust. Now you will have a team of people who can get through to any teenager whenever there's a problem.*

*But wait . . .*

What if all this doesn't work? What if you do everything that I suggested in this book and still no improvement? What if your teenager or student is totally uncoachable? Then what? Well, I don't want to keep you waiting, so let's address the most common questions asked by parents, teachers and even teenagers.

# FAQ by Parents, Teachers and Teenagers

YOU PROBABLY HAVE more specific questions than the ones that I am about to share with you. Keep in mind that these are general questions, but they still apply to the most challenging situations that you go through when it comes to really connecting with them. If you would like to address a specific problem that you're going through with your teen or student, feel free to contact me at Yahya@YahyaBakkar.com for one free 15 minute coaching call.

**The Top 5 Questions Asked By Parents:**

1. How can I get her/him to talk to me?

A: First, you want to acknowledge their space and give them room to breathe. If they're very resistant, approach them when they are at ease and express that you would like to talk about something that's very important to you and it has to do with your fear of _____. Notice I mentioned "your fear" not their problem. In that moment you just broke the barrier and gave them the opportunity to put their guard down.

2.   Why is she/he so argumentative?

**A:** Every behavior stems from a positive intent. Use the framework in chapter 8 (pages 61-64) regarding the six human needs to figure out why he/she is aggressive. Most likely, they will argue to fulfill their needs for certainty, variety, and significance. The interesting thing to realize here is that they will argue when they feel like they aren't being understood. Acknowledge their frustration and empathize with them, then you can get to the heart of the matter. Do this: "I can see why you are _____(mad, upset, angry, etc.), I really wasn't listening to you before. So are you saying that you _____(repeat what they said in your own words so they can guide you to understanding their own world).

3. How do I avoid getting into a power struggle with my teen?

A: GIVE THEM POWER. You will not lose yours. Teenagers today are in the world of control. They control what they see on TV, what they play on the video games, and what they see on the computer. If you are in a power struggle, maintain your composure. Don't get angry or freak out because you couldn't control how they reacted. Lead by example. If you had a lit candle and my candle wasn't lit, you can simply share your light with me and then we will both be lit. That's the true meaning of power. You can both have it at the same time.

4. Why do they suddenly think I'm clueless?

A: It's not because they think you're dumb or that you have no idea what's going on. It's because you weren't able to relate to them. Once you relate to them, then you have gained their trust.

5. Is the tension between us my fault or is it the "teenager" in them?

A: It's no one's fault. The teen's brain is in a state of growth and is establishing neural connections that were never there before. Once you understand this, you will never take it personally again.

**The Top 5 Questions Asked by Teachers:**

1. How can I motivate my students?

A: There aren't any tricks here. Your best bet is to be yourself, have some fun and do something that is unexpected. Once you capture their attention, they will immediately listen to you.

2. What do I do if their parents don't care about their education?

A: This is a tough one. If the parents don't care much about their child's education, then there isn't much you can do. However, you can meet their needs more than their parents, and this usually takes some work. Watch *Freedom Writers* for a great example. If you can find a way to connect with your student and show them that you genuinely care about them, their potential and education, then they will naturally gravitate towards listening to you more than anyone else.

3. How do I handle all the stress that I get from work?

A: Get a massage! Most teachers have amazing healthcare benefits but they never utilize it. Go to a chiropractor, doctor or spa near you and see if you can get a nice hour massage once every two weeks. This does wonders for teachers! Trust me; I was once a massage therapist.

4. What do I do with the students who are disobedient, obnoxious and class clowns?

A: Acknowledge the leader in them. Don't write them off too quick. These students have the potential to be the greatest leaders of the future. The greater the struggle to really get through to them, the greater the positive impact they can have on others once they find someone who only sees their best.

5. What if one of my students is getting bullied? What should I do?

A: Over 75% of teenagers experience bullying or teasing at schools. Bullying is when someone is attacked for who they are, what they do and how they act. This is obviously a serious matter. And let's be honest here, most anti-bullying programs aren't that effective at understanding the root of the problem. Teenagers use bullying as a vehicle to meet their needs and in order for it to be eliminated once and for all, there needs to be a program that educates bullies on how to meet their needs in positive ways. Our nationwide program, The Bullying Cure, is aimed at transforming bullies into positive leaders. This revolutionary program will create a peaceful and powerful paradigm shift within the culture of the school and the lives of the students. For more information visit, www.TheBullyingCure.com.

**The Top 5 Questions Asked by Teens:**

1. Why do they treat me like a child?

**A:** Most teenagers HATE it when they are told what to do. They feel like you don't acknowledge them for the grown-ups they are becoming. Rule of thumb: when you speak to a teenager, talk to them as if they are five years older than what they really are. They want to be respected and you can give them that respect easily by that little switch in perspective.

2. Why don't they just leave me alone?

**A:** I know you care about your teen or student and you just want the best for them. When teenagers say they want to be left alone, that's a sign that you haven't fully connected with them and they are afraid to tell you how they really feel. If they feel that way, say this, "Alright. I will give you your space but I will not drop this subject until we both fully listen to each other. If you are not ready in ____hours/ minutes, I will ask you again. In the meantime, come to me when you are ready to express your point of view."

3. Why don't they trust me?

**A:** I get it. Maybe they lied to you at one point. Maybe it's not them that you don't trust, but it's their friends and the people that are influencing them. You need to express your feelings here. If they feel like you can't trust them, they will play a psychological war with you and you don't want that to happen. Be open minded, show them that you care and get rid of your insecurities that you're possibly projecting on them.

4. Why don't they ever listen to me?

**A:** This is probably the most common question that teenagers ask me. The truth is, it's not that you don't listen; it's that you don't know HOW to listen to them. It's hard to listen to someone who is younger, more inexperienced and doesn't know what they're doing. True or not true? But it's still important to really tune in to their feelings and needs because once you become an effective listener; you automatically become a better leader.

5. Why does everything I want or want to do have to depend on doing chores?

A: Discipline is key. You want to teach them the value of earning something and not just having it placed on their lap. The problem is that when you assign them "responsibilities," they feel like you are just trying to control them and tell them what to do. Feel free to share the reasons behind what you are doing and have healthy discussions about it. For example, "_____, the reason why I ask you to take the garbage out every day is not because I want to punish you, it's because, as a family, we are a team. And as a team we need to make sure we are all carrying our own weight. If I don't work, we wouldn't have food on the table. If mom doesn't _____, we wouldn't _____. If you don't _____, we wouldn't _____. Do you see where I am coming from?"

I hope the answers to these questions have provided you with some value. If you disagree with my approach, please email me. I would love to hear why you disagree and what you've done that has been more effective. My job is to learn, grow and find more effective ways to get through to teens. I am always open to suggestions. Now, let's address the #1 problem that we all must face one way or another.

# The #1 Problem
# We Must Face

I REALLY WISH I had the answers to all of your questions, but I don't. I really wish that this book could solve all your problems, but it won't. I really wish that every single teenager in this world could just behave and live more responsible lives with passion and purpose, but they won't. Maybe it's time for me to just stop wishing for a moment, wake up and face reality. The #1 problem we all must face as human beings is the fact that we don't have all the answers to our most challenging problems. No one does and if someone claims to know everything then they most likely know nothing at all. The only thing we can guarantee one another in this life are the choices we make right now about who we are, who we aspire to become, and what we can do from here on out to help ourselves and those we care about.

My challenge to you is to not be discouraged when connecting to teenagers. Sure they can be disruptive, rude, obnoxious, sarcastic and arrogant at times, but we've all been there before. Remind yourself that they are surfing their way through the waves of life and sometimes they will crash and at other times they will find the right wave and ride it all the way through. The perspective, framework, formula and process that I shared with you in this book are only tools to assist you throughout the hurricanes, tornadoes, tsunamis and the confusing weather forecasts of the teenage years. Don't lose hope. Helping a teenager realize their true gifts can be one of the most rewarding things you'll ever get to experience in your life. Trust that you have what it takes to make a difference and the rest will follow. I hope that this book can serve as a stepping-stone for you. And don't worry, you aren't alone any more. We are partners now and I am here to help you connect with them more effectively than the Internet.

# About the Author

THE OLDEST OF seven siblings, Yahya Bakkar is recognized as one of America's youngest leading authorities on teen life choices, communication and leadership. He is the author of, *The Ultimate Guide to Teen Life* and is a highly sought–after youth speaker and student motivation specialist. Yahya is the founder of *The Bullying Cure*, a nationwide program dedicated to transforming bullies into positive leaders. He is also a 2-time National Jr. Olympic champion in Taekwondo and has trained with the top experts in personal development, relationship dynamics and teen behavior.

Like many people, Yahya faced many challenges growing up.

Born in Makkah, Saudi Arabia, he first traveled alone to the United States at the age of 5.

Abandoned by his biological mother, abused by his father, and mugged in the street at the age of 11, Yahya knows what it feels like to be "dealt the wrong hand."

By overcoming his challenges and continuing to learn from the universal school called "life," Yahya has made it his personal goal to empower teens across the country to reach their potential by breaking through their limiting beliefs and redefining what's possible with their lives.

To learn more, visit: www.YahyaBakkar.com

His fans say, "He's awesome." His friends say, "He's larger than life." His family says, "He's a great role model." Strangers say, "He's like the energizer bunny." Yahya says, "In the end, I'm just one guy who would like to help the next generation help themselves."